TO

_____

FROM

_____

DATE

_____

SIMPLE JOYS
of the AMISH LIFE

MINDY STARNS CLARK *and* GEORGIA VAROZZA
paintings by LAURIE SNOW HEIN

HARVEST HOUSE PUBLISHERS
EUGENE, OREGON

Cover and interior design by Koechel Peterson & Associates, Minneapolis, Minnesota

Unless otherwise indicated, all Scripture quotations are taken from the New King James Version. Copyright © 1982 by Thomas Nelson, Inc. Used by permission. All rights reserved.

Scripture quotations marked (NIV) are taken from the Holy Bible, New International Version®, NIV®. Copyright © 1973, 1978, 1984 by Biblica, Inc.™ Used by permission of Zondervan. All rights reserved worldwide.

Mindy Starns Clark is represented by MacGregor Literary.

Portions of this text adapted from *A Pocket Guide to Amish Life* by Mindy Starns Clark © 2010. Used by permission.

Portions of this text adapted from *The Homestyle Amish Kitchen Cookbook* by Georgia Varozza © 2010. Used by permission.

SIMPLE JOYS OF THE AMISH LIFE

Text copyright © 2011 by Harvest House Publishers

Paintings by © Laurie Snow Hein / Courtesy of Artworks! Licensing

Published by Harvest House Publishers
Eugene, Oregon 97402
www.harvesthousepublishers.com

ISBN 978-0-7369-3003-1

Printed in China

11 12 13 14 15 16 17 18 19 / **FC** / 10 9 8 7 6 5 4 3 2 1

Contents

But may the righteous be glad
and rejoice before God;
may they be happy and joyful.

PSALM 68:3 NIV

THE JOY *of the* AMISH LIFE

Without a doubt, the Amish ignite our curiosity. We buy Amish-made products, cook Amish recipes, read Amish fiction. We take vacations to what we call "Amish country," those Amish-heavy regions like Lancaster County, Pennsylvania, and Holmes County, Ohio. While there, we look for Amish folks from our cars and think about sneaking photographs of them from a distance. We wonder what it would be like to live without constant interruptions, the stress of the rat race, and the intrusions of modern technology. Why are we so curious?

The Amish themselves don't always understand our attraction either, but in response a wise Amish man once issued the following challenge:

If you admire our faith, strengthen yours.

If you admire our sense of commitment, deepen yours.

If you admire our community spirit, build one.

If you admire the simple life, cut back.

If you admire quality merchandise or land stewardship, make quality.

If you admire deep character and enduring values, live them.

This popular saying is frequently posted on the walls of restaurants and tourist attractions in Amish country. The first time I saw it, I understood why its message was so important: We can't all be Amish, but in many ways, we would do well to follow their example.

Living near Lancaster County and interacting regularly with the Amish, I have developed great respect for them over the years. As you enjoy this book, I hope that you will gain a deeper understanding of the Amish faith, life, and values and that you'll enjoy extra insight from the special portions I have labeled *Fascinating Fact*, *Takeaway Value*, and *In Their Own Words*.

Most of all, my prayer is that you will use this knowledge to enhance your own faith. Thus, may we all be "iron sharpening iron"—Amish, author, and reader—helping each other to grow through a new perspective.

Enjoy!

Mindy Starns Clark

author, *A Pocket Guide to Amish Life*

> *Give us this day our daily bread.*
>
> MATTHEW 6:11

⁓

I come from a long line of good cooks, Plain and otherwise, and many of the recipes in this book have been handed down in my family for generations. Other recipes were gleaned from friends at the Conservative Amish Mennonite Church I attended.

For as long as I can remember, the women in my family (and even some of the men) have enjoyed time spent in the kitchen preparing meals for those we love. Some of these recipes weren't written down, but instead were passed down as the daughters worked alongside mothers, learning by doing. Certainly, that's how my sisters and I learned, and by the time we were teens, we were knowledgeable and efficient in the kitchen, and we loved turning out goodies on a weekly basis.

Family lore has it that during the Depression our grandmother issued a standing invitation to the extended family. Every week after church, the whole clan gathered at her table for a big meal. Sometimes this was the only good meal some of the relatives could look forward to all week, and Grandmother always made sure to send home plenty of leftovers with the aunts and uncles and cousins. Because my grandparents lived on a farm, they were able to be generous in spite of the lean times. Mama said they were as poor as church mice right along with everyone else, but food was plentiful, and they were openhanded.

In this fast-paced world, few things are better than taking the time to prepare the ingredients for a great meal and gathering the family around the table to enjoy the results. For a short while, our cares and responsibilities fade into the background, and we can focus on our families, delighting in the small news of the day and savoring the pleasure that comes from a lovingly prepared home-cooked meal. I hope that some of the recipes in this book will find a place in your kitchen, and that as you prepare your family meals, you too will take pleasure in the simple art of cooking for loved ones.

Blessings!

Georgia Varozza
author, *The Homestyle Amish Kitchen Cookbook*

⁓

And do not be conformed to this world, but be transformed by the renewing of your mind, that you may prove what is that good and acceptable and perfect will of God.

ROMANS 12:2

THE BLESSINGS
of a SIMPLER WAY

The word *Amish* originally referred to a group of conservative Christians who followed the teachings of a man named Jakob Ammann. Over the years, of course, *Amish* has grown to mean much more—including a faith culture, a way of life, and a set of values—becoming both a proper noun and an adjective.

Most Amish Groups Share These Similarities:

They adhere to a statement of faith known as the Eighteen Articles.

They wear some form of distinctive "plain" clothing.

They worship in each others' homes rather than in church buildings.

They do not connect their houses to public utilities.

They use horses and buggies as their primary means of transportation.

They limit formal education to the eighth grade.

They live in rural areas.

They emphasize an agrarian lifestyle.

They are pacifists.

They choose their religious leaders through divine appointment by drawing lots.

They speak a German dialect as their primary language.

They value the history of their people and their martyrs' heritage.

Fascinating Fact

The Amish call the non-Amish *English* because we speak English as our primary language instead of the German dialect they use.

By keeping to themselves, the Amish find strength through solidarity for their way of life. Despite their edict to be separate, however, the Amish have friendships with the non-Amish. As one Amish man says, "We treasure friendships of all kinds provided that our respective identities are not challenged and ripped down." Amish businesses also interact with non-Amish businesses on a regular basis.

One of the core elements of the Amish faith is that Christians are to be in the world but not of the world. Many Amish practices are based on this principle, both in the ways they separate themselves from their non-Amish surroundings and in the ways they turn toward each other as a faith community.

In Their Own Words

"For the Amish, culture and religion are intertwined to the point where it is hard to separate the two. Indeed, it is a faith culture."

Georgia's Amish Table Tidbit

The morning meal is important for Amish families. It must feed them and keep them going for many hours of steady work because the noonday meal is a long way off. The breakfast table is also the place where the adults discuss their plans and schedules for the day, where scholars fuel themselves for the hours of learning ahead, and where the first silent prayer of the day is shared by all.

Without a word, Father bows his head, and the family follows. Again without a word, Father begins to serve himself from the many plates and bowls on the table. Prayer time is over. Now it's time to dig in and eat up.

Breakfast is served!

Homemade Graham "Nuts" Cereal

3½ cups whole wheat flour
1 cup brown sugar
1 teaspoon salt
1 teaspoon baking soda
1 teaspoon ground cinnamon
2 cups buttermilk
2 teaspoons vanilla

In a large bowl, combine all ingredients and mix well. Pour out onto an oiled 12 x 16-inch flat, low-sided baking pan and spread evenly with a spatula. Bake at 350° for 20 minutes or until the batter is firm and medium brown and has begun to shrink away slightly from the sides of the pan. With a metal spatula, completely loosen the hot patty and allow to cool on a rack for several hours.

Preheat oven to 275°. Break patty into chunks and put through a meat grinder or a food processor until coarse crumbs are formed. Divide crumbs between two 12 x 16-inch pans.

Bake for 30 minutes, stirring every 10 minutes. Let cool and then store in airtight containers.

Serve as a cold cereal with milk.

Oatmeal Pancakes

2 cups rolled oats
2 cups buttermilk
½ cup unbleached white flour
½ cup whole wheat flour
2 teaspoons sugar
1½ teaspoons baking powder
1½ teaspoons baking soda
1 teaspoon salt
2 eggs
2 tablespoons butter,
melted and cooled slightly

Start preparing these pancakes the night before. In a mixing bowl, combine the oats and buttermilk. Cover and refrigerate overnight.

The next morning, in another mixing bowl, sift together the flours, sugar, baking powder and soda, and salt. Set aside.

In a large mixing bowl, whisk the eggs until they are light and frothy. Add the melted butter and mix together. Next, add the oatmeal/buttermilk mixture and mix well. Blend in the flour mixture with a wooden spoon—at this point the mixture will be very thick. If it appears too dry, you can add a few more tablespoons of buttermilk.

Fry the pancakes in a small amount of vegetable oil, cooking well on both sides. These pancakes really puff up. You can serve them hot from the griddle with butter and maple syrup, but they are also excellent plain.

Homemade Maple Syrup

1 pound brown sugar
½ cup white sugar
1 cup water
⅔ cup light Karo syrup
2 teaspoons maple flavoring

Combine all ingredients and heat until dissolved. Keep leftover syrup in refrigerator. If it crystallizes in the refrigerator, heat gently to dissolve the sugar when next used.

She brings her food from afar.
She also rises while it is yet night,
And provides food for her household...
A woman who fears the LORD, she shall be praised.
Give her the fruit of her hands,
And let her own works praise her in the gates.

PROVERBS 31:14-15,30-31

THE LOVE *of* FAMILY *and* CHILDREN

An Amish childhood is ideally filled with God, love, work, fun, and family—often all at the same time. Unlike modern Americans, the Amish do not strongly delineate between work time and playtime. Instead, they often combine the two, creating a hardworking and satisfying lifestyle. With such large families and close-knit communities, someone always seems to be available to share the load, the learning, and the laughter.

The Amish take parenting very seriously, and when children are growing up, an enormous amount of time is invested in teaching them, guiding them by example, and working with them. As one Amish father says, "I could do this a lot faster by myself, but how else is he going to learn?"

Amish husbands and wives generally assume traditional male-female roles in the family. The husband is typically the breadwinner, and the wife cares for the home and the children. Mothers generally do not work outside of the home unless absolutely necessary.

FASCINATING FACT

Though the Amish don't have telephones in their homes, most do have access to a phone nearby. Often, several neighbors will share a single phone line that connects to a phone booth in a central location. This way, they are able to keep frivolous calls to a minimum, prevent disruptions to family time, and keep their homes "off the grid" while still having access to telephone service.

Amish schoolhouses are usually large enough to accommodate 25 to 30 children of various grade levels, with separate boys' and girls' outhouse-style bathrooms outside. Each school has one teacher, usually an unmarried Amish woman in her late teens or early twenties who has been chosen because of her Christian character, Amish values, and teaching ability. Two-room schoolhouses or single-room schoolhouses with more than 30 children may have a second teacher or a teacher's assistant. Older students often help with the younger students. In schools for Amish children with special needs, the teacher-student ratio is about one to four.

TAKEAWAY VALUE

The National PTA has published a list titled "The Top 10 Things Teachers Wish Parents Would Do." Not surprisingly, the Amish have already been doing many of these things for years, such as setting a good example and encouraging students to do their best. Number ten, however, is central to the way Amish parents operate: "Accept your responsibility as parents. Don't expect the school and teachers to take over your obligations...Teach children self-discipline and respect for others at home—don't rely on teachers and schools to teach these basic behaviors and attitudes."

The Amish would never dream of leaving parental matters such as those described above in the hands of teachers. Instead, they know they are the primary authority figures in their children's lives and are responsible to raise them up in the way that they should go. We would do well to follow their example in this matter—for the sake of our children, their classmates, and their teachers.

Potato Rivvel Soup

3 pounds potatoes, peeled and cubed
½ cup onion
pinch of salt
2 tablespoons butter
salt and pepper
1 cup milk
1 cup water
***rivvels* (recipe follows)**

Put potatoes and onions in a large kettle with water to barely cover and a pinch of salt and cook until the potatoes are done. Do not drain the water. Use a potato masher to mash the potatoes in the water until they are roughly mashed and still lumpy. Then add the butter and salt and pepper to taste.

Next, add the liquid—you need to use a combination of milk and water because the milk gives the soup a creamy richness. Bring the soup to a gentle bubbling simmer. Make the *rivvels*.

Rivvels

1 cup flour
½ teaspoon salt
1 egg

In a medium bowl, mix the flour and salt. Break the egg into the flour mixture and mix together until you have lumps about the size of grapes. This is a fairly messy process, so feel free to use your hands to mix. Drop these *rivvels* into the soup and, stirring occasionally, cook them until done, about 10 minutes or so, depending on their size. If the soup is too thick, you can add more milk. Adjust the seasoning to taste before serving.

Tomato Gravy

¼ cup onion, diced small
2 tablespoons bacon drippings
3 tablespoons flour
1½ cups tomato juice or canned stewed
tomatoes including liquid, chopped fine
½ cup milk or light cream
2 teaspoons brown sugar
salt and pepper to taste

Cook onion in bacon drippings until the onion turns golden.

Add the flour and stir constantly for 30 seconds. Add the tomato juice or tomatoes and liquid in a steady stream, stirring constantly. Next, add the milk or light cream and brown sugar and continue to stir until mixture thickens. Salt and pepper to taste.

Surrounded by family members and farm animals, Amish children often seem to have an endless supply of coworkers and playmates. By pitching in on the farm, children learn responsibility and develop a strong work ethic.

Amish or not, it's hard to imagine children who wouldn't enjoy caring for their very own animals and living in a tightly knit community, surrounded by parents and siblings who love them and willingly spend time with them.

When a couple's children are grown, they might pass down the farm to one of the younger generation and move themselves into the *Grossdaadi Haus*, a smaller house that is connected to or nearby the main house, much like an "in-law suite." There, the elder parents live out the rest of their lives, helping out with the younger ones when they can, providing wisdom and companionship to the family, and growing old with dignity and grace.

GEORGIA'S AMISH TABLE TIDBIT

The Amish believe that "children are a heritage from the Lord," and many families have ten or more children. That's a lot of hungry mouths to feed, and a steaming bowl of hot soup or hearty stew will help satisfy the hunger of growing bodies. Soups are healthy, tasty, and economical, and they are often found at Amish tables, especially during the colder winter months. In summer, fruit soup is enjoyed at mealtime. Often the fruit used in the dinner soup is whatever was processed in the kitchen that day.

Scrapple

1½ pounds ground pork
5 cups water, divided
1 teaspoon salt
½ teaspoon sage
1 cup cornmeal

Break up the ground pork into small pieces in a large saucepan. Add 4 cups of the water and stir, separating the pork well. Heat to boiling, reduce to simmer, and cook 30 minutes. Remove meat from stock, reserve 3 cups of the stock, and add to it salt and sage.

Combine the cornmeal with 1 cup cold water (or a combination of water and milk, which will make the scrapple brown better when fried). Add this cornmeal/water mixture gradually to the hot stock. Bring to a boil, reduce to simmer, cover, and cook 15 minutes. Stir in cooked ground pork. Pour into a loaf pan (9½ x 5 x 3 inches) and chill well for 24 hours. Slice ¼ to ½ inch thick. Fry pieces in hot oil quickly, turning only once. Allow room in the pan to turn. Serve hot either plain, with Tomato Gravy, or with syrup.

The LORD is my shepherd;
I shall not want.
He makes me to lie down in green pastures;
He leads me beside the still waters.
He restores my soul;
He leads me in the paths of righteousness
For His name's sake.

PSALM 23:1-3

THE SIGNIFICANCE *of* FAITH

The Amish are Christians and adhere to these tenets of the Christian faith:

There is one God.

God is a trinity.

Jesus came to earth as God in the flesh, died, and rose again.

Salvation comes through grace by faith.

Scripture is the divinely inspired word of God.

The church is the body of Christ.

As foreign as many Amish practices are to most people, their faith culture is a Christian one. The Amish are not a cult, they do not try to earn grace by their lifestyle, and they do believe in salvation. Feeling that it would be prideful to claim an assurance of that salvation, however, most Amish districts prefer that their members maintain what they call a "living hope" or a "continued effort" on the topic, trusting the ultimate fate of their soul to God's providence rather than claiming it with certainty.

To best understand Amish life, it helps to grasp the basic values that guide almost every facet of their faith. The Amish...

- *surrender* the self-will to God
- *submit* to authority, to the faith community, and to its rules
- *separate* from the world and become a "peculiar people" by turning to family and the faith community, by honoring history and tradition, and by turning the other cheek
- *simplify* through the practice of humility, modesty, thrift, and peacefulness

Jesus lived surrender, submission, separation, and simplicity throughout His life and thus provided the perfect example of these values in action.

IN THEIR OWN WORDS

"The nice thing is that anyone can choose to be a follower of Christ regardless of his lot in life and the cultural context he lives in. No need to be Amish in order to believe in the Lord and have eternal life—unless, of course, the Lord wants you to be Amish."

Church Cinnamon Rolls

³/₄ cup sugar
¹/₃ cup butter, warmed
1 can evaporated milk, warmed
3 tablespoons active dry yeast
3 eggs
4 cups flour (plus more as needed)
1 tablespoon salt
³/₄ cup butter, softened
2 to 3 cups sugar
cinnamon
raisins and nuts, if desired

Put the ³/₄ cup sugar, ¹/₃ cup butter, evaporated milk, and yeast in a large stand mixer and let stand for 5 minutes. Then turn on mixer and mix these ingredients together. Add the eggs, and while mixing, slowly add the 4 cups of flour and tablespoon of salt. Continue adding flour until dough leaves the sides of the bowl. Continue kneading for ten minutes and then place in a large, oiled bowl, cover with a towel, and let rise until doubled.

On a floured surface, roll out dough and spread with ³/₄ cup butter, 2 to 3 cups sugar, and lots of cinnamon. You can also spread on nuts or raisins if desired.

Roll dough into a log and cut into 2 dozen rolls. Place cut side up on 2 greased jelly roll pans, cover with a towel, and let rise again.

Bake in a preheated oven at 350° for 25 minutes or until done.

For this recipe, I place the butter and evaporated milk in a small saucepan and gently warm them on the stove. Just be careful that the mixture doesn't get too hot.

Stewed Tomatoes and Dumplings

Stewed Tomatoes

¼ cup butter
½ cup onion, finely chopped
¼ cup celery, chopped
1 28-ounce can whole tomatoes,
coarsely chopped, with juice
2 teaspoons brown sugar
½ teaspoon salt
½ teaspoon dried basil
¼ teaspoon pepper

Dumplings

1 cup flour
1½ teaspoons baking powder
½ teaspoon salt
1 tablespoon butter
1 egg, beaten
6 tablespoons milk
1 tablespoon fresh parsley, minced

In a medium saucepan, melt the butter and sauté the onion and celery about 3 minutes. Add the tomatoes and juice, brown sugar, and seasonings, and bring to a boil. Simmer uncovered for several minutes.

In a mixing bowl, combine the flour, baking powder, and salt for the dumplings. Cut in the butter using a pastry blender or two knives until the mixture resembles coarse cornmeal. Add the egg, milk, and parsley and blend lightly. Do not overmix. Drop dumplings by tablespoonfuls on top of the simmering tomato mixture. Cover tightly and cook over medium low heat for 20 minutes. Do not lift the cover during the cooking period.

Serve in bowls, topped with butter if desired.

You can also use 2 quarts of home-canned stewed tomatoes for this recipe instead of the 28-ounce can. It yields more sauce, which works just fine in this recipe.

TAKEAWAY VALUE

We should strive for Christlikeness in all that we do, even if in practice that may look different for us than it does for the Amish.

Most elements of the Amish lifestyle that seem unique or confusing relate not to some complicated or controversial theology but instead to the way they have chosen to live out their Christian walk in their day-to-day lives. They attempt to follow the teachings of Jesus, particularly the Sermon on the Mount, by emphasizing certain values. Though outsiders may think the Amish take some of these principles to the extreme, the tenets of their faith are based on the Bible.

GEORGIA'S AMISH TABLE TIDBIT

What aroma could possibly be more soothing than the delicious scent of homemade bread rising and baking! Large Amish families eat many loaves of bread in a week, and women commonly bake as many as a dozen loaves at a time. Bread baking is an art form as much as a culinary skill, and Amish women take great care when baking their loaves, learning from their mothers how the dough feels when it has been kneaded long enough, how high to raise the dough, and the perfect oven temperature for producing a loaf of bread that is high but doesn't fall, with small air pockets and a moist interior.

Amish Dressing

4 eggs
½ teaspoon salt
⅛ teaspoon pepper
½ teaspoon sage
½ teaspoon thyme
3½ to 4 cups milk, as needed
1 medium onion, finely chopped
3 stalks celery, finely chopped
¾ cup cooked potatoes, chopped
2 cups cooked chicken, chopped
½ cup cooked carrots, finely diced
1 loaf bread, diced and toasted

Put the eggs into a bowl and beat them. Mix in the salt, pepper, sage, and thyme. Add 2 cups milk, onion, celery, potatoes, chicken, and carrots. Add the bread with enough milk to moisten it well.

Bake in a well-greased casserole dish at 350° for 1½ hours or until the dressing has an omelet-like texture but is not too dry.

Be devoted to one another in brotherly love. Honor one another above yourselves. Never be lacking in zeal, but keep your spiritual fervor, serving the Lord. Be joyful in hope, patient in affliction, faithful in prayer. Share with God's people who are in need. Practice hospitality.

ROMANS 12:10-13 NIV

THE UNITY
of COMMUNITY

The community is the cornerstone of Amish life. It is where they most often find their identity, support, lifestyle, worship, classmates, spouses, and friends. It is a source of strength, an insurance policy when disaster strikes, and a safe haven in an often hostile (or at least intrusively curious) world.

To the outsider, this strong sense of community is one of the most appealing aspects of Amish life. Who wouldn't want the safety net of a loving group of friends and relatives to surround them during bad times, celebrate together in good times, and bear the ups and downs of life together? The very thought sounds like music to our culturally isolated ears.

This is the Amish view of community:

Everyone in the community is accountable to God.

The virtue of humility is shown through respect for God and others.

All persons are worthy of dignity and respect.

Communities are made stronger when individuals do not use personal desire as their supreme criteria for making decisions.

Traditions are more important than progress.

Accumulated wisdom is better than an individual's ideas.

Authority in all of its various forms is to be obeyed.

A *district* is a group of Amish who live near each other and worship together, somewhat like a congregation or a parish. Districts average about 135 people (20 to 40 families), and as membership and families grow, new districts are created by dividing existing districts.

An *affiliation* is a collection of districts with similar lifestyle regulations and cooperative relationships among their leaders. Affiliations are not defined by geography but by practices and beliefs. Roughly 25 different Amish affiliations exist in the United States and Canada.

TAKEAWAY VALUE

Surrounded by a community of believers, one can always find friendship, fellowship, comfort, help, accountability, and more.

GEORGIA'S AMISH TABLE TIDBIT

Salads are often made using ingredients from the family garden, but the Amish are also fond of Jell-O salads for special occasions as well as hearty potato and macaroni salads that can feed many. In early spring, Amish children forage for dandelion greens to make a tasty salad that is rumored to cleanse the blood, which has turned sluggish from the long winter.

Layered Salad

1 head of lettuce, torn into pieces
1 cup celery, diced
4 hard-boiled eggs, diced
3 cups peas, cooked
½ cup bell pepper, diced
1 medium sweet onion, diced
8 slices bacon, cooked, cooled, and torn into small pieces
2 cups mayonnaise
2 tablespoons sugar
4 ounces Cheddar cheese, grated

Using a 9 x 12-inch dish, layer the first seven ingredients. Mix the mayonnaise and sugar together until well blended and then spread over the top of the other ingredients, as if you were frosting a cake. Go all the way to the edges, being careful to seal all edges. Sprinkle on the grated cheese. Set in refrigerator for 8 to 12 hours. At serving time, you can garnish with some fresh parsley and more bacon pieces if desired.

Haystack Supper

This recipe makes enough for two casseroles, so divide the ingredients into two baking dishes.

40 saltine crackers, crushed
2 cups cooked rice
3 pounds hamburger
1 large onion, chopped
1½ cups tomato juice
¾ cup water
3 tablespoons taco seasoning
salt and pepper to taste
4 cups lettuce, shredded
3 medium tomatoes, diced
½ cup butter, cubed
½ cup flour
4 cups milk
1 pound Velveeta cheese, cubed
3 cups sharp Cheddar cheese, shredded
1 can pitted olives
1 package tortilla chips (14½ ounces)

Divide the crackers between two ungreased 13 x 9-inch baking dishes. Top each with rice.

In a large skillet, brown the hamburger and onion; drain. Add the tomato juice, water, and seasonings and simmer for 20 minutes. Spoon meat mixture over rice. Next, layer on the lettuce and tomatoes.

In a large saucepan, melt the butter. Stir in the flour and continue stirring until smooth. Gradually add the milk. Continue stirring, bring to a boil, and cook until the sauce thickens, about 2 minutes. Reduce heat to low and stir in Velveeta cheese until melted. Pour cheese mixture over the lettuce and tomatoes. Top with Cheddar cheese and olives and serve with the tortilla chips.

German Potato Salad

8 potatoes, peeled, cubed, and boiled
1 stalk celery, chopped
2 hard-boiled eggs
1 onion, chopped
1 tablespoon fresh parsley, minced

Combine all ingredients in a large bowl and then prepare dressing.

Dressing

4 slices bacon, diced
2 eggs, well beaten
1 cup sugar
½ cup vinegar
½ cup cold water
¼ teaspoon dry mustard
½ teaspoon salt
¼ teaspoon pepper

Fry the bacon in a skillet until crisp. Remove the bacon bits and add to salad. Beat together eggs, sugar, vinegar, water, and spices. Pour mixture into the hot bacon grease and cook, stirring until mixture thickens, about 10 minutes. Pour over the potato mixture and mix lightly. Refrigerate for several hours before serving.

When you eat the labor of your hands,
You shall be happy, and it shall be well with you.

PSALM 128:2

THE GIFT
of HARD WORK

More hands make lighter work, or so the saying goes. The Amish have this principle down to a science and frequently share the load when doing tedious tasks. For example, adult sisters often meet once a month at each other's houses for what they call a *frolic*, which is simply a gathering together to visit with each other while doing chores such as canning food, shucking corn, cleaning house, and more. By rotating houses, they help each other out, get their own work done, and have fun all at the same time. Amish women also gather together for quilting parties.

Perhaps the biggest symbol of community in action is the well-known Amish barn raising. These events involve hundreds of Amish working together for a single day. In about nine hours, they can construct an oak beam-and-peg barn that will last for generations. The Amish use their barns for farmwork, storing feed and grain, sheltering livestock, and housing valuable farm tools. Barns are also social centers where church services, funerals, marriages, and baptisms may be held.

To the outsider, the extent to which members of the Amish community care for each other is often mind-boggling. To the Amish, it is simply one of the primary values that define their lives.

TAKEAWAY VALUE

Organizing a work frolic is a great idea regardless of whether you're Amish! Consider joining together with a group of friends or relatives once a month to spend a few hours doing tedious household chores and visiting as you work. The jobs will get done faster, and you'll enjoy a great visit at the same time. Rotate to a different house each month so everyone's home gets a turn.

From a very early age, Amish children are taught that working hard is a vitally important virtue, and they are expected to learn how to plan and cook meals, guide a horse and buggy, plow the fields, and more. On Amish farms, young children may be given a small animal such as a chicken, duck, or goat that they alone must care for, which instills a strong work ethic and a sense of responsibility. They are also taught basic business principles, and older children may even derive a small income from their own produce stand or other home-based business. If children want something, they are encouraged to work for it, as the Amish believe that a gift given too easily too soon robs children of the joy of earning it for themselves.

These days, *Amish* is also a marketing buzzword and can be seen on everything from jars of jam to space heaters to backyard sheds and swing sets. Some outsiders use the Amish moniker to cash in on a reputation for quality, value, and integrity. Exploitative or not, those implications provide high praise to the ones who bear its title and live out its principles day after hardworking day.

Yum-a-Setta

This makes a great potluck dish.

2 pounds hamburger
salt and pepper to taste
2 tablespoons brown sugar
¼ cup onion, chopped
1 can tomato soup
1 16-ounce package egg noodles
1 can cream of chicken soup
1 cup Velveeta cheese

Brown hamburger with salt, pepper, brown sugar, and onion; drain off grease. Add tomato soup to the meat mixture and mix.

Meanwhile, cook the egg noodles according to package directions; drain. Add cream of chicken soup to the noodles and mix.

Layer hamburger mixture and noodle mixture in a 13 x 9-inch casserole dish with Velveeta cheese between layers. Bake at 350° for 30 minutes.

Poor Man's Steak

1 pound hamburger
1 cup milk
1 cup cracker crumbs
1/4 teaspoon pepper
1 teaspoon salt
1 small onion, chopped
1 can cream of mushroom soup
1/2 can water

Combine all ingredients except the soup and water. Mix well and shape into a narrow loaf. Refrigerate at least 8 hours or overnight. Cut into slices and fry in a skillet on both sides until brown.

Put the slices of meat close together in a roasting pan. Mix together the soup and water and spread over the meat slices. Bake at 325° for 1 hour.

The Amish believe that setting limits and respecting them are keys to Christlikeness, wisdom, and fulfillment. To them, regulations shape identity, build community, help prevent temptation, and provide a sense of belonging. Without rules, they feel, one can fall prey to pride, unhappiness, insecurity, loss of dignity, and ultimately self-destruction.

Limitations on Amish life are dictated by the *Ordnung*, which is what the Amish call the unwritten set of rules and regulations that dictates their day-to-day life. The *Ordnung* deals with a wide variety of topics, such as clothing, transportation, technology, education, and much more.

GEORGIA'S AMISH TABLE TIDBIT

Casseroles are a good answer for what to feed the family on busy days. Simply mix together the ingredients and pop the dish into a slow-burning oven to simmer and bake for hours. When the family returns from their day, the aroma from the kitchen beckons them to hurry and take their places at the table. The Amish family waits for Father to bow his head and lead the family in silent prayer—then it's time to enjoy what Mother and the girls have prepared.

A typical dinner might consist of Yum-a-Setta, potatoes and carrots from the garden, sliced fresh tomatoes, home-canned applesauce, and cookies and pie for dessert. Water and coffee are often the beverages of choice.

German Dark Rye Bread

3 cups regular flour
4½ teaspoons (2 packages) active dry yeast
¼ cup baking cocoa powder
1 tablespoon caraway seeds
2 cups water
⅓ cup molasses
2 tablespoons butter
1 tablespoon sugar
1 tablespoon salt
3 to 3½ cups rye flour

In large mixing bowl, combine regular flour, yeast, cocoa powder, and caraway seeds until well blended.

In a saucepan, combine the water, molasses, butter, sugar, and salt; heat until just warm, stirring occasionally to melt butter. Add to dry mixture. Beat at low speed for 30 seconds and then turn to higher speed and beat for 3 minutes more.

By hand, stir in enough rye flour to make a soft dough. Turn out onto floured surface and knead until smooth (about 5 minutes), adding more rye flour as needed. Cover; let stand for 20 minutes.

Punch down and divide dough in half. Shape each half into a round loaf; place on greased baking sheets or two greased pie plates. Brush surface of loaves with a little cooking oil. Slash tops of loaves with a sharp knife. Let rise until double, about 45 to 60 minutes.

Bake at 400° for 25 to 30 minutes or until bread looks done. Remove from baking pans and cool on wire racks.

THE VALUE *of* CELEBRATIONS *and* CEREMONIES

Despite the common use of the term—even in this book—there's actually no such thing as an "Amish child." The more correct wording would be "child of Amish parents" or "child in an Amish community." That's because people aren't *born* Amish; they must *become* Amish, which is a voluntary process that happens at the cusp of adulthood, usually in the late teens or early twenties. That's when those who have been raised in Amish homes decide whether they are going to accept the Amish faith and be baptized into its membership.

Before that, however, every Amish teen experiences *Rumspringa*, which is Pennsylvania Dutch for "running around." The goal of *Rumspringa* is to relax the rules a bit, to allow teenagers to experience a taste of the outside world, to find a mate (they hope), and to give them enough freedom to make an informed, independent, and mature decision about whether they want to be baptized and become Amish like their parents or instead leave the Amish faith and forge a new life on their own.

When a young person decides he wants to be baptized, he presents himself for the first of eight or nine classes taught over the course of several months. Baptisms occur only once a year, so many parents of teens hold their breath, waiting to see if their children are among those who choose to attend the class.

Like their non-Amish counterparts, Amish children enter first grade around age six. School hours and term lengths are similar to those in public school, though the Amish generally don't take as much time off for holidays. In Lancaster County, for example, Christmas is only a two-day break. Their school year ends in early May.

Amish weddings can be quite large, often with 300 to 500 guests. The Amish don't use caterers, so the food preparation alone can be a tremendous undertaking. Fortunately, plenty of volunteers are always available to help out, and the communities have been through so many weddings before that everyone is familiar with the various duties required.

Weddings are usually held in the bride's parents' home, barn, or shop. The regular Sunday benches are used, though if the wedding is large, benches from several other nearby communities may be needed as well. In a carefully orchestrated event, family and friends work to prepare the wedding feast and ready the home for the celebration.

An Amish wedding ceremony is similar in many ways to a regular Amish Sunday worship service. As the congregation sings the opening hymns, the couple is brought into a separate room with the bishop and ministers for a time of "admonition and encouragement" called the *Abroth*. This lasts about 20 or 30 minutes, and then all rejoin the congregation for the rest of the service. As on Sundays, an opening sermon, a prayer, a Bible reading, and a main sermon are included. The bride and groom each have two attendants. In most districts, the couple wears brand-new versions of their usual Sunday attire, with one exception: The groom sports his first "real" Amish hat, one with a broader brim to indicate that he is married.

FASCINATING FACT

In some regions, despite all of the secrecy regarding courtships, nosy community members can usually figure out which families will be having a fall wedding by the amount of celery they've planted in their garden that year. Celery is a late-growing vegetable, so it's a common fixture at weddings both as a main food and in table decorations. If the guest list will be large, as it usually is, the celery must be grown in great quantities, far more than a family would otherwise need.

Amish Wedding Nothings

1 egg
³/₄ cup cream
pinch of salt
2 to 3 cups flour
shortening or lard for deep frying
powdered sugar for sprinkling

Beat the egg and then stir in the cream, salt, and enough flour to make a stiff dough. Divide the dough into seven balls and roll each ball flat and very thin. Cut three 2-inch slits through the middle of the circle of dough.

Heat the shortening in a deep fryer to 365°. Fry one piece at a time, turning over with two forks when it turns light golden.

Take out when done and drain on paper towels. Sprinkle with powdered sugar. Stack nothings on top of each other, sprinkling with powdered sugar each time you add another to the stack.

Christmas Cake

1 pound butter
1 pound light brown sugar
6 eggs
4 cups flour, sifted
1 teaspoon baking powder
2 tablespoons nutmeg
½ cup orange juice
3 cups chopped pecans
1 pound pale yellow seedless raisins

Cream together the butter and sugar. Add the eggs, two at a time, and beat until very light and the mixture doesn't look grainy (this takes about 20 or 25 minutes). Sift together the flour, baking powder, and nutmeg. Add gradually to the creamed mixture and beat until well blended. Stir in the orange juice or blend in using lowest speed on mixer. Fold in the pecans and raisins.

Pour the cake batter into a 10-inch tube (bundt) pan that has been greased and floured. Bake at 300° for 1 hour and 45 minutes.

Remove from oven and cool for 10 minutes. Then turn the pan over and let cake slip out gently. Cool completely. Wrap tightly and store for at least a week before serving because it tends to be crumbly when fresh.

Most Amish folks accept death gracefully. They consider it the ultimate submission to God, the surrender of the living body to the grave. Amish or not, dealing with death is never easy, but being surrounded by an ever-present group of believers in times of grief can be a great comfort and aid.

When an Amish person dies, news spreads throughout the community primarily by word of mouth. In response, Amish friends and neighbors spring into action, helping with funeral arrangements, farm and household chores, and the preparation of the home for the funeral.

GEORGIA'S AMISH TABLE TIDBIT

Every year, my father bought handmade fruitcake from the Trappist monks. I knew it was meant to be a special treat, but I didn't care for it. After many years, I found the courage to tell my father, and he laughed and said he didn't like fruitcake either, but he felt Christmas wouldn't be complete without it. Fortunately, Christmas Cake makes a tasty stand-in for the more traditional recipe.

Funeral Pie

1 double-crust pie pastry, unbaked
2 cups raisins
2 cups water, divided
½ cup brown sugar
½ cup granulated sugar
3 tablespoons cornstarch
1½ teaspoons cinnamon
¼ teaspoon allspice
pinch of salt
1 tablespoon cider vinegar
3 tablespoons butter

Line a pie pan with half the pastry and set in refrigerator to chill.

Place the raisins and ⅔ cup of the water in a saucepan and heat over medium heat for 5 minutes.

Combine sugars, cornstarch, cinnamon, allspice, and salt in a bowl. Continue mixing while slowly adding the remaining water. Add this mixture to the heating raisins. Cook and stir this until the mixture begins to bubble. Add the vinegar and butter and heat just until the butter is melted. Remove from heat and allow mixture to cool a bit. Pour into the prepared pie shell and top with the second crust.

Bake for 25 minutes at 400° or until golden. The pie will set up more as it cools.

Popcorn Birthday Cake

12 cups popped corn (unsalted)
1 12-ounce package peanuts,
no paper skins
6 tablespoons butter
1 10.5-ounce bag marshmallows
1 teaspoon vanilla
½ teaspoon salt
1 12-ounce package mini M&Ms

Generously butter a tube (bundt) pan and set aside. Place the popcorn and peanuts in a very large mixing bowl.

In a saucepan over low heat, melt the butter and marshmallows together, stirring constantly so the mixture doesn't burn. Add the vanilla and salt and stir to blend. Immediately pour the mixture over the popcorn. Butter your hands and mix with your hands quickly. Add the M&Ms and finish mixing, still using your hands. Press firmly into the prepared cake pan and let stand for at least 1 hour.

When ready to serve, unmold the cake onto a serving plate and add candles.

Better is a little with righteousness,
Than vast revenues without justice...
Pleasant words are like a honeycomb,
Sweetness to the soul and health to the bones.

PROVERBS 16:8,24

THE SWEETNESS
of HUMILITY

The Amish put tremendous emphasis on the Christian value of humility and go to great lengths to prevent the sin of pride in every area of their lives. They do this in many ways, for example by discouraging individuality, limiting formal education, and emphasizing selflessness.

The uniformity of Amish clothing encourages humility and reflects other important Amish values as well, such as thrift, modesty, and community.

FASCINATING FACT

The oldest surviving Amish settlement is in Lancaster County, Pennsylvania. The largest Amish settlement is in and around Holmes County, Ohio.

The Amish emphasis on Christlikeness is expressed through clothing in several ways:

Humility: Dressing alike provides less opportunity for vanity.

Submission: Following the clothing rules of the district demonstrates obedience to God, to the group, and to history.

Denial of self: Dressing alike prevents individuality and pride.

Simplicity: Limiting clothing choices saves time and effort.

Modesty: Prescribed styles guarantee propriety.

Thrift: Making clothes, especially from limited fabric and pattern choices, saves money, as does the lack of jewelry and clothing accessories.

Chocolate Sauerkraut Cake

1 16-ounce can sauerkraut,
rinsed and well drained
²/₃ cup butter
1½ cups sugar
3 eggs
2 teaspoons vanilla
½ cup unsweetened baking
cocoa powder
1 teaspoon baking powder
1 teaspoon salt
1 teaspoon baking soda
2¼ cups flour
1 cup cold water

Using your hands, squeeze out as much moisture from the kraut as possible. Chop it finely and set aside.

In a large mixing bowl, beat together the butter and sugar until light and fluffy. Add the eggs, one at a time, beating well after each addition. Add the vanilla, cocoa powder, baking powder, salt, and baking soda; blend well. Add the flour alternately with the water. Fold in the sauerkraut until well incorporated.

Pour into a greased 13 x 9-inch baking pan and bake at 350° for 30 minutes or until done. When cool, frost with chocolate frosting or cut when slightly warm and serve with whipped cream.

Shoo-Fly Pie

1 cup molasses
½ cup brown sugar
2 eggs, beaten
1 cup hot water
1 teaspoon baking soda,
dissolved in hot water
2 8-inch unbaked pie crusts
2 cups flour
³/₄ cup brown sugar
⅓ cup butter
½ teaspoon cinnamon

Mix the first five ingredients thoroughly together to make a syrup. Divide mixture in half and pour into the two unbaked pie shells. Thoroughly mix together the rest of the ingredients for a crumb topping. Divide and sprinkle crumb topping onto the two pies.

Bake at 450° for 10 minutes and then reduce heat to 350° and continue baking until done, about another 30 minutes.

TAKEAWAY VALUE

Few of us would choose to limit our clothing options as severely as the Amish have, but something can be said for the simplicity of the Amish way of dressing. Think about the amount of time you spend on clothing—shopping for it, coordinating outfits, cleaning it, storing it, finding the right shoes and the right accessories, and so on. Imagine, then, how it would feel to wake up and face a simple closet or row of clothing pegs, knowing that your only choice is between three colors of the same dress. Many days, I wish I could have such a streamlined wardrobe and spend my time on far more important matters!

Specifics can vary from district to district, but all Amish clothing is modest, loose fitting, and of a predetermined style and choice of colors. Head coverings are worn every day by men, women, and teens. Children wear head coverings in church and at school, though not always in more casual settings, depending on district rules.

In deference to teachings in 1 Corinthians, Amish women never cut their hair but instead allow it to grow. They consider a woman's hair to be her glory, which she shares only with her husband in private. Otherwise, Amish women part their hair in the middle, pull it tightly back, and fasten it into a bun or braid. Prayer coverings are worn over the hair. In general, the less conservative a district, the smaller the female's head covering.

For everyday wear, Amish men usually sport dark broadfall trousers with a flap that buttons at the waist. These are worn with suspenders. In the interest of modesty, suspenders allow for a looser fit, and in the interest of humility, they supplant belt buckles, which are considered fancy.

GEORGIA'S AMISH TABLE TIDBIT

The Amish are well-known for their desserts—especially pies—and the assortment of recipes is astounding. Pastry-making is an acquired skill, and Amish girls learn early how to turn out a good pie. The trick to good crusts is to measure carefully and handle quickly and gently.